MW01206562

Personal Explorations Workbook

FOR WEITEN AND LLOYD'S
Psychology Applied to Modern Life

Wayne Weiten
Santa Clara University

Wadsworth
Thomson Learning

Australia • Canada • Mexico • Singapore • Spain • United Kingdom • United States

Sponsoring Editor: Eileen Murphy
Assistant Editor: Annie Berterretche
Printing and Binding: D.B. Hess

COPYRIGHT © 2000 Wadsworth, a division of
Thomson Learning. Thomson Learning is a trademark
used herein under license.

ALL RIGHTS RESERVED. No part of this work
covered by the copyright hereon may be reproduced or
used in any form or by any means—graphic,
electronic, or mechanical, including photocopying,
recording, taping, Web distribution, or information
storage and retrieval systems—without the prior
written permission of the publisher.

Printed in the United States of America

6 7 8 9 10 11 12 07 06 05 04

For permission to use material from this text,
contact us by **Web:** http://wwwthomsonrights.com
Fax: 1-800-730-2215 **Phone:** 1-800-730-2214

ISBN 0-534-36665-1

For more information, contact
Wadsworth/Thomson Learning
10 Davis Drive
Belmont, CA 94002-3098
USA
http://www.wadsworth.com

International Headquarters
Thomson Learning
International Division
290 Harbor Drive, 2nd Floor
Stamford, CT 06902-7477
USA

UK/Europe/Middle East/South Africa
Thomson Learning
Berkshire House
168-173 High Holborn
London WC1V 7AA
United Kingdom

Asia
Thomson Learning
60 Albert Complex, #15-01
Singapore 189969

Canada
Nelson Thomson Learning
1120 Birchmount Road
Toronto, Ontario M1K 5G4
Canada

CONTENTS

In your textbook, *Psychology Applied to Modern Life* the value of developing an accurate self-concept is emphasized repeatedly. A little self-deception may occasionally be adaptive, (see Chapter 4 in your text), but most theories of psychological health endorse the importance of forming a realistic picture of one's personal qualities and capabilities. The *Personal Explorations Workbook* designed to accompany your text contains two types of exercises intended to help you achieve this goal. They are (1) a series of Personal Probes intended to help you systematically analyze various aspects of your life, and (2) a series of Questionnaires or self-scoring psychological scales intended to help you gain insight into your attitudes and personality traits.

How you use these personal exploration exercises will depend, in large part, on your instructor. Many Instructors will formally assign some of these exercises and then collect them, either for individual scrutiny or class discussion. That is why the pages of this book are perforated–to make it convenient for those instructors who like to assign the exercises as homework. Other instructors may simply encourage students to complete the exercises that they find intriguing. We believe that even if the exercises are not assigned, you will find many of them to be very interesting, and we encourage you to complete them on your own. Let's briefly take a closer look at these exercises.

QUESTIONNAIRES

The Questionnaires are a collection of attitude scales and personality tests that psychologists have used in their research. One Questionnaire has been selected for each chapter in your text. Instructions are provided so that you can administer these scales to yourself and then compute your score. Each Questionnaire also includes an explanation of what the scale measures, followed by a brief review of the research on the scale. These reviews discuss the evidence on the reliability, validity, and behavioral correlates of each scale. The final section of each Questionnaire provides information to allow you to interpret the meaning of your score. Test norms are supplied to indicate what represents a high, intermediate, or low score on the scale. We hope you may gain some useful insights about yourself by responding to these scales.

However, you should be careful about attributing too much significance to your scores. As explained in the Application for Chapter 2 in your text, the results of psychological tests can be misleading, and caution is always in order when interpreting test scores. It is probably best to view your scores as interesting "food for thought", rather than as definitive statements about your personal traits or abilities.

Most of the scales included in this book are self-report inventories. Your scores on such tests are only as accurate as the information that you provide in your responses. Hence, we hasten to emphasize that these Questionnaires will only be as valuable as you make them, by striving to respond honestly. Usually, people taking a scale do not know what the scale measures. The conventional approach is to put some sort of vague or misleading title, such as "Biographical Inventory," at the top of the scale. We have not adhered to this practice because you could easily find out what any scale measures simply by reading ahead a little. Thus, you will be taking each scale with some idea (based on the title) of what the scale measures. Bear in mind, however, that these scales are intended to satisfy your curiosity. There is no reason to try to impress or mislead anyone–including yourself. Your test scores will be accurate and meaningful only if you try very hard to respond in a candid manner.

PERSONAL PROBES

The Personal Probes consist of sets of questions designed to make you think about yourself and your personal experiences in relation to specific issues and topics raised in your text. They involve systematic inquiries into how you behave in certain situations, how your behavior has been shaped by past events, how you feel about certain issues, how you might improve yourself in some areas, and so forth. There is one Personal Probe for each of the 16 chapters in your textbook. The aspects of life probed by these inquiries are, of course, tied to the content of the chapters in your text. You will probably derive the most benefit from them if you read the corresponding text chapter before completing the Personal Probe.

Testwiseness Scale

INSTRUCTIONS

Below you will find a series of 24 history questions for which you are *not* expected to know the answer based on your knowledge of history. However, you should be able to make a good guess on each of the questions if you can spot the flaws that exist in them. Each question is flawed in some way so as to permit solution by testwise examinees. Record your choice for each question by circling the letter for the correct alternative.

THE SCALE

1. The Locarno Pact

   a. is an international agreement for the maintenance of peace through the guarantee of national boundaries of France, Germany, Italy, Belgium, and other countries of Western Europe.
   b. allowed France to occupy the Ruhr Valley.
   c. provided for the dismemberment of Austria-Hungary.
   d. provided for the protection of Red Cross bases during wartime.

2. The disputed Hayes-Tilden election of 1876 was settled by an

   a. resolution of the House of Representatives.
   b. decision of the United States Supreme Court.
   c. Electoral Commission.
   d. joint resolution of Congress.

3. The Factory Act of 1833 made new provisions for the inspection of the mills. This new arrangement was important because

   a. the inspectors were not local men and therefore they had no local ties that might affect the carrying-out of their job; they were responsible to the national government rather than to the local authorities; and they were encouraged to develop a professional skill in handling their work.
   b. the inspectorate was recruited from the factory workers.
   c. the inspectors were asked to recommend new legislation.
   d. the establishment of the factory inspectorate gave employment to large numbers of the educated middle class.

4. The Ostend Manifesto aimed to

   a. discourage Southern expansionism.
   b. prevent expansion in the South.
   c. aid Southern expansionism.
   d. all of the above

5. The august character of the work of Pericles in Athens frequently causes his work to be likened to that in Rome of

   a. Augustus.
   b. Sulla.
   c. Pompey.
   d. Claudius.

6. The Webster-Ashburton Treaty settled a long-standing dispute between Great Britain and the United States over

   a. the Maine boundary.
   b. numerous contested claims to property as well as many other sources of ill will.
   c. damages growing out of the War of 1812 and subsequent events.
   d. fishing rights on the Great Lakes and in international waters.

7. Men who opposed the "Ten Hour Movement" in British factory history

   a. was a leader in the dominant political party.
   b. is convinced that shorter hours of work are bad for the morals of the laboring classes.
   c. is primarily motivated by concern for his own profits.
   d. were convinced that intervention would endanger the economic welfare of Britain.

8. The career of Marius (157–86 B.C.), the opponent of Sulla, is significant in Roman history because

   a. he gave many outstanding dinners and entertainments for royalty.
   b. he succeeded in arming the gladiators.
   c. he showed that the civil authority could be thrust aside by the military.
   d. he made it possible for the popular party to conduct party rallies outside the city of Rome.

9. The Locarno Pact

   a. was an agreement between Greece and Turkey.
   b. gave the Tyrol to Italy.
   c. was a conspiracy to blow up the League of Nations building at Locarno.
   d. guaranteed the boundary arrangements in Western Europe.

10. The first presidential election dispute in the United States to be settled by an appointed Electoral Commission was

    a. the Hayes-Tilden election.
    b. the Jefferson-Madison election.
    c. the John Quincy Adams-Henry Clay election.
    d. the Garfield-McKinley election.

11. The first of the alliances against the "Central Powers" that ended in World War I is to be found in

    a. the defensive treaty between China and Japan.
    b. the dual alliance of Mexico and the United States.
    c. the dual alliance of France and Russia.
    d. India's resentment against South Africa's attitude toward the Boer War, and her ensuing alliance with Japan.

12. The Proclamation of 1763

    a. forbade colonists to settle territory acquired in the French and Indian wars.
    b. encouraged colonists to settle territory acquired in the French and Indian wars.
    c. provided financial incentives for settlement of territory acquired in the French and Indian wars.
    d. all of the above

13. About what fraction of the 1920 population of the United States was foreign-born?

    a. less than 5%
    b. between 14% and 28%
    c. 25%
    d. between 30% and 50%

14. The Alabama claims were

    a. all settled completely and satisfactorily.
    b. claims against Jefferson Davis for seizure of all of the property in the state during wartime.
    c. claims of the United States against Great Britain.
    d. claims of every citizen of Alabama against every citizen of Georgia.

15. During the Italian Renaissance

    a. the papacy gained political power.
    b. there were frequent changes in government.
    c. the papacy became more important in Italian political affairs.
    d. all of the above

16. The 12th century was distinguished by a "real European patriotism" that expressed itself in

    a. the flowering of lyrical and epical poetry in the vernacular.
    b. great patriotic loyalty to the undivided unit of European Christendom.
    c. recurring attempts to form a world with a centralized administration.
    d. proposals to remove the custom barriers between the different countries of the time.

17. The dispute between Great Britain and the United States over the boundary of Maine was settled by

    a. the Treaty of Quebec.
    b. the Treaty of Niagara.
    c. the Webster-Ashburton Treaty.
    d. the Pendleton-Scott Treaty.

18. In the *Dartmouth College* case the United States Supreme Court held

    a. that the courts had no right under any circumstances ever to nullify an Act of Congress.
    b. that a state could not impair a contract.
    c. that all contracts must be agreeable to the state legislature.
    d. that all contracts must inevitably be certified.

19. The accession of Henry VII marked the close of the

    a. Crusades
    b. War of the Roses, between rival factions of the English nobility.
    c. Hundred Years' War.
    d. Peasants' Revolt.

20. The Magna Carta was signed

    a. before the Norman invasion.
    b. in 1215.
    c. after the opening of the 17th century.
    d. about the middle of the 14th century.

21. The Progressive Party in 1912

    a. favored complete protective tariffs.
    b. favored an appointed Congress.
    c. favored the creation of a nonpartisan tariff commission.
    d. favored restriction of the ballot to certain influential persons.

22. The first systematic attempt to establish the Alexandrian synthesis between Christian religious belief and Greek civilization was undertaken at

    a. Rome.
    b. Alexandria.
    c. Athens.
    d. Jerusalem.

23. The Bland-Allison Act

    a. made all forms of money redeemable in silver.
    b. standardized all gold dollars in terms of silver and copper.
    c. made none of the paper money redeemable in silver.
    d. directed the Treasury Department to purchase a certain amount of silver bullion each month.

24. The famed Bayeaux Tapestry is a

    a. enormous re-creation of the Magna Carta scene.
    b. extremely large impression of the Edict of Nantes.
    c. immense picture of the Battle of Tours.
    d. large representation of the Norman Conquest of England.

SCORING THE SCALE

There are eight item-writing flaws that appear on the Testwiseness Scale three times each. They are described below.

Flaw #1: The incorrect options are highly implausible.

Flaw #2: Equivalence and/or contradictions among options allow one to eliminate the incorrect options.

Flaw #3: Content information in other items provides the answer.

Flaw #4: The correct option is more detailed and/or specific than all the other options.

Flaw #5: The correct option is longer than all of the other options.

Flaw #6: There is grammatical inconsistency between the stem and the incorrect options but not the correct option.

Flaw #7: The incorrect options include certain key words that tend to appear in false statements (such as *always, must, never,* and so on).

Flaw #8: There is a resemblance between the stem and the correct option but not the incorrect options.

The scoring key is reproduced below. For each item it tells you the correct answer and indicates which flaw (as numbered above) you should have spotted to arrive at the answer. Circle those items that you got correct. Add up the number of correct items, and that is your score on the Testwiseness Scale. Record your score below.

1. A (5)	**7.** D (6)	**13.** C (4)	**19.** B (5)
2. C (6)	**8.** C (1)	**14.** C (7)	**20.** B (4)
3. A (5)	**9.** D (3)	**15.** D (2)	**21.** C (1)
4. C (2)	**10.** A (3)	**16.** B (8)	**22.** B (8)
5. A (8)	**11.** C (1)	**17.** C (3)	**23.** D (7)
6. A (4)	**12.** A (2)	**18.** B (7)	**24.** D (6)

MY SCORE_____

WHAT THE SCALE MEASURES

As its title indicates, this scale simply measures your ability to reason your way to answers on multiple-choice exams. The Testwiseness Scale (TWS) assesses test-taking skills. The scale you have just completed is an abbreviated version of a scale developed by Wayne Weiten (Weiten, Clery, & Bowbin, 1980). The full scale is a 40-item test with five items for each kind of flaw.

The TWS is built on some pioneering work by Gibb (1964). Through a series of revisions, reliability and validity have gradually been improved. The full-length version yields internal reliability coefficients in the .70s and .80s. Two lines of evidence currently provide support for the scale's validity. First, scores on the scale are very much affected (positively) by training in the principles of testwiseness. Second, as one would expect, the scale correlates positively (.40s) with classroom performance on multiple-choice tests. More important, this correlation between the TWS and classroom performance remains significant even when the influence of intelligence on both variables is factored out statistically.

INTERPRETING YOUR SCORE

Our norms are based on the performance of 76 undergraduates who took the most recent revision of the scale. These norms are for people who have not had any testwiseness training.

NORMS

High score:	17–24
Intermediate score:	9–16
Low score:	0–8

What Are Your Study Habits Like?

Do you usually complete your class assignments on time?   YES   NO

Do you usually find time to prepare adequately for your exams?   YES   NO

Do you frequently delay schoolwork until the last minute?   YES   NO

When do you usually study (mornings, evenings, weekends, etc.)?

Do you write out and follow a study schedule?   YES   NO

Are your study times planned for when you're likely to be alert?   YES   NO

Do you allow time for brief study breaks?   YES   NO

Where do you usually study (library, kitchen, bedroom, etc.)?

Do you have a special place set up for studying and nothing else?   YES   NO

What types of auditory, visual, and social distractions are present in your study areas?

Can you suggest any changes to reduce distractions in your study areas?

Desirability of Control Scale

INSTRUCTIONS

Below you will find a series of statements. Please read each statement carefully and respond to it by expressing the extent to which you believe the statement applies to you. For all items, a response from 1 to 7 is required. Use the number that best reflects your belief when the scale is defined as follows:

1 = The statement does not apply to me at all
2 = The statement usually does not apply to me
3 = Most often, the statement does not apply
4 = I am unsure about whether or not the statement applies to me, or it applies to me about half the time
5 = The statement applies more often than not
6 = The statement usually applies to me
7 = The statement always applies to me

THE SCALE

_____1. I prefer a job where I have a lot of control over what I do and when I do it.

_____2. I enjoy political participation because I want to have as much of a say in running government as possible.

_____3. I try to avoid situations where someone else tells me what to do.

_____4. I would prefer to be a leader than a follower.

_____5. I enjoy being able to influence the actions of others.

_____6. I am careful to check everything on an automobile before I leave for a long trip.

_____7. Others usually know what is best for me.

_____8. I enjoy making my own decisions.

_____9. I enjoy having control over my own destiny.

_____10. I would rather someone else take over the leadership role when I'm involved in a group project.

_____11. I consider myself to be generally more capable of handling situations than others are.

_____12. I'd rather run my own business and make my own mistakes than listen to someone else's orders.

_____13. I like to get a good idea of what a job is all about before I begin.

_____14. When I see a problem, I prefer to do something about it rather than sit by and let it continue.

_____15. When it comes to orders, I would rather give them than receive them.

_____16. I wish I could push many of life's daily decisions off on someone else.

_____17. When driving, I try to avoid putting myself in a situation where I could be hurt by another person's mistake.

_____18. I prefer to avoid situations where someone else has to tell me what it is I should be doing.

_____19. There are many situations in which I would prefer only one choice rather than having to make a decision.

_____20. I like to wait and see if someone else is going to solve a problem so that I don't have to be bothered with it.

SCORING THE SCALE

To score this scale, you must reverse the numbers you entered for five of the items. The responses to be reversed are those for items 7, 10, 16, 19, and 20. For each of these items, make the following conversions: If you entered 1, change it to 7. If you entered 2, change it to 6. If you entered 3, change it to 5. If you entered 4, leave it unchanged. If you entered 5, change it to 3. If you entered 6, change it to 2. If you entered 7, change it to 1.

Now add up the numbers for all 20 items, using the new numbers for the reversed items. This sum is your score on the Desirability of Control Scale. Enter it below.

MY SCORE _____

Source: Burger & Cooper, 1979

WHAT THE SCALE MEASURES

Devised by Jerry Burger and Harris Cooper (1979), the Desirability of Control (DC) Scale measures the degree to which people are motivated to see themselves in control of the events that take place in their lives. In other words, the DC scale basically taps your *need for control*. Burger views the desire for control as a general personality trait, and he has conducted extensive research relating this trait to many aspects of behavior, including social interaction, achievement strivings, gambling, and reactions to stress. Some of the more interesting findings on desire for control, summarized in a recent book (Burger, 1990), include the following. In comparison to those who score low in the desire for control, people who have a high desire for control make more efforts to influence others. According to Burger, it's not that high DC people want to run others' lives; rather they work to influence others in order to exert more control over their own outcomes. Indeed, they appear to be very reluctant to surrender any control over their own lives, and they react more negatively than low DC people when others try to influence them.

In regard to achievement issues, people high in the desire for control tend to set high standards for themselves, and they work extra hard on challenging tasks—to demonstrate their personal mastery and control. How does the desire for control affect gambling habits? The relations between DC and *how much* people gamble are complex, but desire for control does have a fairly consistent effect on which games of chance people prefer to play. High DC people prefer games that offer some perception—perhaps illusory—that one exerts some control over outcomes (blackjack versus roulette, for instance). Who handles stress more effectively? The answer appears to be complex. On the one hand, high DC people seem to do a better job of structuring their lives to avoid stressful, uncontrollable situations. On the other hand, when they are confronted with an uncontrollable situation, high DC people tend to get more upset than those who are low in the desire for control.

INTERPRETING YOUR SCORE

Among older subjects, males tend to score a little higher in desire for control than do females, but gender differences in DC scores are minimal among college students, so we will use a unified set of norms, which are shown below.

NORMS

High score:	111–140
Intermediate score:	90–110
Low score:	20–89

Who Are You?

1. Below you will find 75 personality-trait words taken from the list assembled by Anderson (1968). Try to select the 20 traits (20 only!) that describe you best. Check them.

sincere	forgetful	truthful	imaginative	outgoing
pessimistic	crafty	mature	impolite	dependable
open-minded	methodical	skeptical	diligent	persistent
suspicious	sly	efficient	prideful	orderly
patient	headstrong	resourceful	optimistic	energetic
tense	naive	perceptive	considerate	modest
cooperative	sloppy	punctual	courteous	smart
neat	grouchy	prejudiced	candid	kind
logical	ethical	friendly	idealistic	good-humored
vain	persuasive	gracious	warm	unselfish
sociable	nervous	shy	versatile	cordial
scornful	clumsy	short-tempered	courageous	wholesome
cheerful	rebellious	compulsive	tactful	generous
honest	studious	sarcastic	loyal	boastful
reasonable	understanding	respectful	reliable	daring

2. Review the 20 traits that you chose. Overall, is it a favorable or unfavorable picture that you have sketched?

3. Considering Carl Rogers' point that we often distort reality and construct an overly favorable self-concept, do you feel that you were objective?

4. What characteristics make you unique?

5. What are your greatest strengths?

6. What are your greatest weaknesses?

Sensation-Seeking Scale

INSTRUCTIONS

Each of the items below contains two choices, A and B. Please indicate in the spaces provided on the left which of the choices most describes your likes or the way you feel. It is important that you respond to all items with only one choice, A or B. In some cases you may find that both choices describe your likes or the way you feel. Please choose the one that better describes your likes or feelings. In some cases you may not like either choice. In these cases mark the choice you dislike least. We are interested only in your likes or feelings, not in how others feel about these things or how one is supposed to feel. There are no right or wrong answers. Be frank and give your honest appraisal of yourself.

THE SCALE

_____ 1. A. I would like a job which would require a lot of traveling.
B. I would prefer a job in one location.

_____ 2. A. I am invigorated by a brisk, cold day.
B. I can't wait to get indoors on a cold day.

_____ 3. A. I find a certain pleasure in routine kinds of work
B. Although it is sometimes necessary, I usually dislike routine kinds of work.

_____ 4. A. I often wish I could be a mountain climber.
B. I can't understand people who risk their necks climbing mountains.

_____ 5. A. I dislike all body odors.
B. I like some of the earthy body smells.

_____ 6. A. I get bored seeing the same old faces.
B. I like the comfortable familiarity of everyday friends.

_____ 7. A. I like to explore a strange city or section of town by myself, even if it means getting lost.
B. I prefer a guide when I am in a place I don't know well.

_____ 8. A. I find the quickest and easiest route to a place and stick to it.
B. I sometimes take different routes to a place I often go, just for variety's sake.

_____ 9. A. I would not like to try any drug that might produce strange and dangerous effects on me.
B. I would like to try some of the new drugs that produce hallucinations.

_____ 10. A. I would prefer living in an ideal society where everyone is safe, secure, and happy.
B. I would have preferred living in the unsettled days of our history.

_____ 11. A. I sometimes like to do things that are a little frightening.
B. A sensible person avoids activities that are dangerous.

_____ 12. A. I order dishes with which I am familiar, so as to avoid disappointment and unpleasantness.
B. I like to try new foods that I have never tasted before.

_____ 13. A. I can't stand riding with a person who likes to speed.
B. I sometimes like to drive very fast because I find it exciting.

_____ 14. A. If I were a salesperson, I would prefer a straight salary rather than the risk of making little or nothing on a commission basis.
B. If I were a salesperson, I would prefer working on a commission if I had a chance to make more money than I could on a salary.

_____ 15. A. I would like to take up the sport of water skiing.
B. I would not like to take up the sport of water skiing.

_____ 16. A. I don't like to argue with people whose beliefs are sharply divergent from mine, since such arguments are never resolved.
B. I find people who disagree with my beliefs more stimulating than people who agree with me.

_____ 17. A. When I go on a trip, I like to plan my route and timetable fairly carefully.
B. I would like to take off on a trip with no pre-planned or definite routes or timetables.

_____ 18. A. I enjoy the thrills of watching car races.
B. I find car races unpleasant.

_____ 19. A. Most people spend entirely too much money on life insurance.
B. Life insurance is something that no one can afford to be without.

_____ 20. A. I would like to learn to fly an airplane.
B. I would not like to learn to fly an airplane.

_____ 21. A. I would not like to be hypnotized.
B. I would like to have the experience of being hypnotized.

_____ 22. A. The most important goal of life is to live it to the fullest and experience as much of it as you can.
B. The most important goal of life is to find peace and happiness.

_____ 23. A. I would like to try parachute jumping.
B. I would never want to try jumping out of a plane, with or without a parachute.

_____ 24. A. I enter cold water gradually, giving myself time to get used to it.
B. I like to dive or jump right into the ocean or a cold pool.

_____ 25. A. I do not like the irregularity and discord of most modern music.
B. I like to listen to new and unusual kinds of music.

Source: Zuckerman, 1979

_____26. A. I prefer friends who are excitingly unpre-
dictable.
B. I prefer friends who are reliable and pre-
dictable.

_____27. A. When I go on a vacation, I prefer the comfort
of a good room and bed.
B. When I go on a vacation, I would prefer the
change of camping out.

_____28. A. The essence of good art is in its clarity, sym-
metry of form, and harmony of colors.
B. I often find beauty in the "clashing" colors
and irregular forms of modern paintings.

_____29. A. The worst social sin is to be rude.
B. The worst social sin is to be a bore.

_____30. A. I look forward to a good night of rest after a
long day.
B. I wish I didn't have to waste so much of a day
sleeping.

_____31. A. I prefer people who are emotionally expres-
sive even if they are a bit unstable.
B. I prefer people who are calm and even-tem-
pered.

_____32. A. A good painting should shock or jolt the
senses.
B. A good painting should give one a feeling of
peace and security.

_____33. A. When I feel discouraged, I recover by relaxing
and having some soothing diversion.
B. When I feel discouraged, I recover by going
out and doing something new and exciting.

_____34. A. People who ride motorcycles must have some
kind of an unconscious need to hurt themselves.
B. I would like to drive or ride on a motorcycle.

SCORING THE SCALE
The scoring key is reproduced below. You should circle your
response of A or B each time it corresponds to the keyed
response below. Add up the number of responses you circle.
This total is your score on the Sensation-Seeking Scale.
Record your score below.

1. A	8. B	15. A	22. A	29. B
2. A	9. B	16. B	23. A	30. B
3. B	10. B	17. B	24. B	31. A
4. A	11. A	18. A	25. B	32. A
5. B	12. B	19. A	26. A	33. B
6. A	13. B	20. A	27. B	34. B
7. A	14. B	21. B	28. B	

MY SCORE_____

WHAT THE SCALE MEASURES
As its name implies, the Sensation-Seeking Scale (SSS) measures one's need for a high level of stimulation. Sensation
seeking involves the active pursuit of experiences that many
people would find very stressful. Marvin Zuckerman (1979)
believes that this thirst for sensation is a general personality
trait that leads people to seek thrills, adventures, and new
experiences.

The scale you have just responded to is the second version of
the SSS. Test-retest reliabilities are quite respectable and there
is ample evidence to support the scale's validity. For example,
studies show that high sensation seekers appraise hypotheti-
cal situations as less risky than low sensation seekers and are
more willing to volunteer for an experiment in which they will
be hypnotized. The scale also shows robust positive correlations with measures of change seeking, novelty seeking,
extraversion, and impulsiveness. Interestingly, SSS scores tend
to decline with age.

INTERPRETING YOUR SCORE
Our norms are based on percentiles reported by Zuckerman
and colleagues for a sample of 62 undergraduates. Although
males generally tend to score a bit higher than females on the
SSS, the differences are small enough to report one set of
(averaged) norms. Remember, sensation-seeking scores tend
to decline with age. So, if you're not in the modal college student age range (17–23), these norms may be a bit high.

NORMS
High score:	21–34
Intermediate score:	11–20
Low score:	0–10

Where's the Stress in Your Life?

As you learned in Chapter 3, it's a good idea to be aware of the stress in your life. For this exercise you should keep a stress awareness record for one week. Construct a record sheet like that shown below. About twice a day, fill in the information on any stressful events that have occurred. Under "Type of Stress" indicate whether the event involves frustration, conflict, pressure, change, or some combination.

Day	Time	Stressful Event	Type of Stress	Your Reaction

At the end of the week, answer the following questions.

1. Is there a particular type of stress that is most frequent in your life?

2. Is there a particular locale or set of responsibilities that produces a great deal of stress for you?

3. Are there certain reactions to stressful events that you display consistently?

4. Is there anything reasonable that you could do to reduce the amount of stress in your life?

Barnes–Vulcano Rationality Test

INSTRUCTIONS

For each of the following statements, please indicate the degree to which you tend to either agree or disagree with the statement according to the following five-point scale:

1	2	3	4	5
Agree Strongly	Agree	Neither Agree nor Disagree	Disagree	Disagree Strongly

THE SCALE

_____1. I do not need to feel that everyone I meet likes me.

_____2. I frequently worry about things over which I have no control.

_____3. I find it easy to overcome irrational fears.

_____4. I can usually shut off thoughts that are causing me to feel anxious.

_____5. Life is a ceaseless battle against irrational worries.

_____6. I frequently worry about death.

_____7. Crowds make me nervous.

_____8. I frequently worry about the state of my health.

_____9. I tend to worry about things before they actually happen.

_____10. If I were told that someone had a criminal record I would not hire him or her to work for me.

_____11. When I make a mistake I feel worthless and inadequate.

_____12. When someone is wrong I sure let them know.

_____13. When I am frustrated the first thing I do is ask myself whether there is anything I can do to change it now.

_____14. Whenever something goes wrong I ask myself, "Why did this have to happen to me?"

_____15. Whenever things go wrong I say to myself, "I don't like this, I can't stand it."

_____16. I usually find a cure for my own depression when it occurs.

_____17. Once I am depressed it takes me a long while to recover.

_____18. I feel that when I become depressed or unhappy it is caused by other people or the events that happen.

_____19. People have little or no ability to control their sorrows or rid themselves of their negative feelings.

_____20. When I become angry I usually control my anger.

_____21. I can usually control my appetite for food and alcohol.

_____22. The value of a human being is directly proportionate to her/his accomplishments; if s/he is not thoroughly competent and adequate in achieving s/he might as well curl up and die.

_____23. The important part of playing the game is that you succeed.

_____24. I feel badly when my achievement level is lower than others'.

_____25. I feel that I must succeed at everything I undertake.

_____26. When I feel doubts about potential success I avoid participating and risking the chance of failure.

_____27. When I set out to accomplish a task I stick with it to the end.

_____28. If I find difficulties in life I discipline myself to face them.

_____29. If I try to do something and encounter problems I give up easily.

_____30. I find it difficult to work at tasks that have a long-range payoff.

_____31. I usually like to face my problems head on.

_____32. A person never learns from his/her mistakes.

_____33. Life is what you make it.

_____34. Unhappy childhoods inevitably lead to problems in adult life.

_____35. I try not to brood over past mistakes.

_____36. People who are selfish make me mad because they really should not be that way.

_____37. If I had to nag someone to get what I wanted I would not think it was worth the trouble.

_____38. I frequently find that life is boring.

_____39. I often wish that something new and exciting would happen.

_____40. I experience life as just the same old thing from day to day.

_____41. I often wish life were more stimulating.

_____42. I often feel that everything is tiresome and dull.

_____43. I wish I could change places with someone who lives an exciting life.

_____44. I often wish life were different than it is.

Source: Barnes & Vulcano, 1982

SCORING THE SCALE

To score this scale, you must reverse the numbers you entered for 12 of the items. The responses to be reversed are those for items 1, 3, 4, 13, 16, 20, 21, 27, 28, 31, 33, and 35. For each of these items, make the following conversions: If you circled 1, change it to 5. If you circled 2, change it to 4. If you circled 3, leave it unchanged. If you circled 4, change it to 2. If you circled 5, change it to 1.

Now add up the numbers for all 44 items, using the new numbers for the reversed items. This sum, which should fall somewhere between 44 and 220, is your score on the Barnes–Vulcano Rationality Test. Enter it below.

MY SCORE_____

WHAT THE SCALE MEASURES

Devised by Gordon Barnes and Brent Vulcano (1982), the Barnes–Vulcano Rationality Test (BVRT) measures the degree to which people do or do not subscribe to the irrational assumptions described by Albert Ellis (1962, 1973). As Chapter 4 in your text explains, Ellis believes that troublesome emotions and overreactions to stress are caused by negative self-talk or catastrophic thinking. This catastrophic thinking is thought to be derived from irrational assumptions that people hold. The items on the BVRT are based on 10 of the irrational assumptions described by Ellis, such as the idea that one must receive love and affection from certain people, or the idea that one must be thoroughly competent in all endeavors. The scale is set up so that high scores indicate that one tends to think relatively rationally, whereas low scores indicate that one is prone to the irrational thinking described by Ellis. The BVRT has excellent reliability, and the authors took steps to minimize contamination from social desirability bias. Evidence regarding the test's validity can be gleaned from various correlational analyses. For example, high scores on the BVRT have been found to correlate negatively with measures of neuroticism (–.50), depression (–.55), and fear (–.31), indicating that respondents who score high on the test tend to be less neurotic, depressed, or fearful than others.

INTERPRETING YOUR SCORE

Our norms, which are shown below, are based on combined data from two sets of adults studied by Barnes and Vulcano (1982). The first sample consisted of 172 subjects (with a mean age of 22), and the second included 177 subjects (with a mean age of 27).

NORMS

High score:	166–220
Intermediate score:	136–165
Low score:	44–135

Can You Detect Your Irrational Thinking?

You should begin this exercise by reviewing the theories of Albert Ellis. To briefly recapitulate, Ellis believes that unpleasant emotional reactions are caused not by events themselves, but by catastrophic interpretations of events derived from irrational assumptions. It is therefore important to detect and dispute these catastrophic modes of thinking. Over a period of a week or so, see if you can spot two examples of irrational thinking on your part. Describe these examples as requested below.

EXAMPLE NO. 1
Activating event:

Irrational self-talk:

Consequent emotional reaction:

Irrational assumption producing irrational thought:

More rational, alternative view:

EXAMPLE NO. 2
Activating event:

Irrational self-talk:

Consequent emotional reaction:

Irrational assumption producing irrational thought:

More rational, alternative view:

Self-Monitoring Scale

INSTRUCTIONS

The statements below concern your personal reactions to a number of situations. No two statements are exactly alike, so consider each statement carefully before answering. If a statement is true or mostly true as applied to you, mark T as your answer. If a statement is false or not usually true as applied to you, mark F as your answer. It is important that you answer as frankly and as honestly as you can. Record your responses in the spaces provided on the left.

THE SCALE

_____ 1. I find it hard to imitate the behavior of other people.

_____ 2. My behavior is usually an expression of my true inner feelings, attitudes, and beliefs.

_____ 3. At parties and social gatherings, I do not attempt to do or say things that others will like.

_____ 4. I can only argue for ideas I already believe.

_____ 5. I can make impromptu speeches even on topics about which I have almost no information.

_____ 6. I guess I put on a show to impress or entertain people.

_____ 7. When I am uncertain how to act in a social situation, I look to the behavior of others for cues.

_____ 8. I would probably make a good actor.

_____ 9. I rarely need the advice of my friends to choose movies, books, or music.

_____10. I sometimes appear to others to be experiencing deeper emotions than I actually am.

_____11. I laugh more when I watch a comedy with others than when alone.

_____12. In a group of people I am rarely the center of attention.

_____13. In different situations and with different people, I often act like very different persons.

_____14. I am not particularly good at making other people like me.

_____15. Even if I am not enjoying myself, I often pretend to be having a good time.

_____16. I'm not always the person I appear to be.

_____17. I would not change my opinions (or the way I do things) in order to please someone else or win their favor.

_____18. I have considered being an entertainer.

_____19. In order to get along and be liked, I tend to be what people expect me to be rather than anything else.

_____20. I have never been good at games like charades or improvisational acting.

_____21. I have trouble changing my behavior to suit different people and different situations.

_____22. At a party, I let others keep the jokes and stories going.

_____23. I feel a bit awkward in company and do not show up quite so well as I should.

_____24. I can look anyone in the eye and tell a lie with a straight face (if for a right end).

_____25. I may deceive people by being friendly when I really dislike them.

SCORING THE SCALE

The scoring key is reproduced below. You should circle your response of true or false each time it corresponds to the keyed response below. Add up the number of responses you circle. This total is your score on the Self-Monitoring Scale. Record your score below.

1. False	2. False	3. False	4. False	5. True	6. True	7. True	8. True	9. False	10. True
11. True	12. False	13. True	14. False	15. True	16. True	17. False	18. True	19. True	20. False
21. False	22. False	23. False	24. True	25. True					

MY SCORE_____

Source: Snyder, 1974

WHAT THE SCALE MEASURES

Developed by Mark Snyder (1974), the Self-Monitoring (SM) Scale measures the extent to which you consciously employ impression management strategies in social interactions. Basically, the scale assesses the degree to which you manipulate the nonverbal signals that you send to others and the degree to which you adjust your behavior to situational demands. As we discussed, some people work harder at managing their public images than do others.

In his original study, Snyder (1974) reported very reasonable test-retest reliability (.83 for one month) and, for an initial study, provided ample evidence regarding the scale's validity. In assessing the validity of the scale, he found that in comparison to low SM subjects, high SM subjects were rated by peers as being better at emotional self-control and better at figuring out how to behave appropriately in new social situations. Furthermore, Snyder found that stage actors tended to score higher on the scale than undergraduates, as one would expect. Additionally, Ickes and Barnes (1977) summarize evidence that high SM people are (1) very sensitive to situational cues, (2) particularly skilled at detecting deception on the part of others, and (3) especially insightful about how to influence the emotions of others.

INTERPRETING YOUR SCORE

Our norms are based on guidelines provided by Ickes and Barnes (1977). The divisions are based on data from 207 undergraduate subjects.

NORMS

High score:	15–22
Intermediate score:	9–14
Low score:	0–8

How Does Your Self-Concept Compare to Your Self-Ideal?

Below you will find a list of 15 traits, each portrayed on a 9-point continuum. Mark with an X where you think you fall on each trait. Try to be candid and accurate; these marks will collectively describe a portion of your self-concept. When you are finished, go back and circle where you wish you could be on each dimension. These marks describe your self-ideal. Finally, in the spaces on the right, indicate the size of the discrepancy between self-concept and self-ideal for each trait.

1. Decisive   Indecisive   _____
   9   8   7   6   5   4   3   2   1

2. Anxious   Relaxed   _____
   9   8   7   6   5   4   3   2   1

3. Easily influenced   Independent thinker   _____
   9   8   7   6   5   4   3   2   1

4. Very intelligent   Less intelligent   _____
   9   8   7   6   5   4   3   2   1

5. In good physical shape   In poor physical shape   _____
   9   8   7   6   5   4   3   2   1

6. Undependable   Dependable   _____
   9   8   7   6   5   4   3   2   1

7. Deceitful   Honest   _____
   9   8   7   6   5   4   3   2   1

8. A leader   A follower   _____
   9   8   7   6   5   4   3   2   1

9. Unambitious   Ambitious   _____
   9   8   7   6   5   4   3   2   1

10. Self-confident   Insecure   _____
    9   8   7   6   5   4   3   2   1

11. Conservative   Adventurous   _____
    9   8   7   6   5   4   3   2   1

12. Extraverted   Introverted   _____
    9   8   7   6   5   4   3   2   1

13. Physically attractive   Physically unattractive   _____
    9   8   7   6   5   4   3   2   1

14. Lazy   Hardworking   _____
    9   8   7   6   5   4   3   2   1

15. Funny   Little sense of humor   _____
    9   8   7   6   5   4   3   2   1

Overall, how would you describe the discrepancy between your self-concept and your self-ideal (large, moderate, small, large on a few dimensions)?

How do sizable gaps on any of the traits affect your self-esteem?

Do you feel that any of the gaps exist because you have had others' ideals imposed on you or because you have thoughtlessly accepted others' ideals?

Argumentativeness Scale

INSTRUCTIONS

This questionnaire contains statements about arguing controversial issues. Indicate how often each statement is true for you personally by placing the appropriate number in the blank to the left of the statement:

1	2	3	4	5
Almost never true	Rarely true	Occasionally true	Often true	Almost always true

THE SCALE

_____ 1. While in an argument, I worry that the person I am arguing with will form a negative impression of me.

_____ 2. Arguing over controversial issues improves my intelligence.

_____ 3. I enjoy avoiding arguments.

_____ 4. I am energetic and enthusiastic when I argue.

_____ 5. Once I finish an argument I promise myself that I will not get into another.

_____ 6. Arguing with a person creates more problems for me than it solves.

_____ 7. I have a pleasant, good feeling when I win a point in an argument.

_____ 8. When I finish arguing with someone I feel nervous and upset.

_____ 9. I enjoy a good argument over a controversial issue.

_____10. I get an unpleasant feeling when I realize I am about to get into an argument.

_____11. I enjoy defending my point of view on an issue.

_____12. I am happy when I keep an argument from happening.

_____13. I do not like to miss the opportunity to argue a controversial issue.

_____14. I prefer being with people who rarely disagree with me.

_____15. I consider an argument an exciting intellectual challenge.

_____16. I find myself unable to think of effective points during an argument.

_____17. I feel refreshed and satisfied after an argument on a controversial issue.

_____18. I have the ability to do well in an argument.

_____19. I try to avoid getting into arguments.

_____20. I feel excitement when I expect that a conversation I am in is leading to an argument.

SCORING THE SCALE

Add up the numbers that you have recorded for items 1, 3, 5, 6, 8, 10, 12, 14, 16, and 19. This total reflects your tendency to avoid getting into arguments. Next, add up the numbers that you have recorded for items 2, 4, 7, 9, 11, 13, 15, 17, 18, and 20. This total reflects your tendency to approach argumentative situations. Record these subtotals in the spaces below. Subtract your avoidance score from your approach score to arrive at your overall score.

_____ − _____ = _____

Approach score   Avoidance score   Total score

Source: Infante & Rancer, 1982

WHAT THE SCALE MEASURES

This questionnaire measures an aspect of your social influence behavior. Specifically, it assesses your tendency to argue with others in persuasive efforts. Persons who score high on this scale are not bashful about tackling controversial issues, are willing to attack others verbally to make their points, and are less compliant than the average person. Developed by Infante and Rancer (1982), this scale has high test-retest reliability (.91 for a period of one week). Examinations of the scale's validity show that it correlates well with other measures of communication tendencies and with friends' ratings of subjects' argumentativeness.

INTERPRETING YOUR SCORE

Our norms are based on the responses of over 800 undergraduate subjects studied by Infante and Rancer (1982).

NORMS

High score:	16 and above
Intermediate score:	–6 to 15
Low score:	–7 and below

Can You Identify Your Prejudicial Stereotypes?

1. List and briefly describe examples of three prejudicial stereotypes that you hold or have held at one time.

Example 1:

Example 2:

Example 3:

2. Try to identify the sources (family, friends, media, etc.) of each of these stereotypes.

Example 1:

Example 2:

Example 3:

3. For each stereotype, how much actual interaction have you had with the stereotyped group, and has this interaction affected your views?

Example 1:

Example 2:

Example 3:

4. Can you think of any ways in which the fundamental attribution error or defensive attribution has contributed to these stereotypes?

Fundamental attribution error:

Defensive attribution:

Opener Scale

INSTRUCTIONS

For each statement, indicate your degree of agreement or disagreement, using the scale shown below. Record your responses in the spaces on the left.

4 = I strongly agree

3 = I slightly agree

2 = I am certain

1 = I slightly disagree

0 = I strongly disagree

THE SCALE

_____ 1. People frequently tell me about themselves.

_____ 2. I've been told that I'm a good listener.

_____ 3. I'm very accepting of others.

_____ 4. People trust me with their secrets.

_____ 5. I easily get people to "open up."

_____ 6. People feel relaxed around me.

_____ 7. I enjoy listening to people.

_____ 8. I'm sympathetic to people's problems.

_____ 9. I encourage people to tell me how they are feeling.

_____10. I can keep people talking about themselves.

SCORING THE SCALE

This scale is easy to score! Simply add up the numbers that you have recorded in the spaces on the left. This total is your score on the Opener Scale.

MY SCORE_____

WHAT THE SCALE MEASURES

Devised by Lynn Miller, John Berg, and Richard Archer (1983), the Opener Scale is intended to measure your perception of your ability to get others to "open up" around you. In other words, the scale assesses your tendency to elicit intimate self-disclosure from people. The items assess your perceptions of (a) others' reactions to you ("People feel relaxed around me"), (b) your interest in listening ("I enjoy listening to people"), and (c) your interpersonal skills ("I can keep people talking about themselves").

In spite of its brevity, the scale has reasonable test-retest reliability (.69 over a period of six weeks). Correlations with other personality measures were modest, but in the expected directions. For instance, scores on the Opener Scale correlate positively with a measure of empathy and negatively with a measure of shyness. Further evidence for the validity of the scale was obtained in a laboratory study of interactions between same-sex strangers. Subjects who scored high on the scale compared to those who scored low elicited more self-disclosure from people who weren't prone to engage in much disclosure.

INTERPRETING YOUR SCORE

Our norms are based on the original sample of 740 undergraduates studied by Miller, Berg, and Archer (1983). They found a small but statistically significant difference between This exercise is intended to make you think about your self-disclosure behavior. Begin by finishing the incomplete sentences below (adapted from Egan, 1977). Go through the sentences fairly quickly; do not ponder your responses too long. There are no right or wrong answers.

NORMS

	Females	Males
High score:	35–40	33–40
Intermediate score:	26–34	23–32
Low score:	0–25	0–22

Source: Miller, Berg, & Archer, 1983

WHAT THE SCALE MEASURES

This questionnaire measures an aspect of your social influence behavior. Specifically, it assesses your tendency to argue with others in persuasive efforts. Persons who score high on this scale are not bashful about tackling controversial issues, are willing to attack others verbally to make their points, and are less compliant than the average person. Developed by Infante and Rancer (1982), this scale has high test-retest reliability (.91 for a period of one week). Examinations of the scale's validity show that it correlates well with other measures of communication tendencies and with friends' ratings of subjects' argumentativeness.

INTERPRETING YOUR SCORE

Our norms are based on the responses of over 800 undergraduate subjects studied by Infante and Rancer (1982).

NORMS

High score: 16 and above

Intermediate score: –6 to 15

Low score: –7 and below

How Do You Feel About Self-Disclosure?

This exercise is intended to make you think about your self-disclosure behavior. Begin by finishing the incomplete sentences below (adapted from Egan, 1977). Go through the sentences fairly quickly; do not ponder your responses too long. There are no right or wrong answers.

1. I dislike people who . . .

2. Those who really know me . . .

3. When I let someone know something I don't like about myself . . .

4. When I'm in a group of strangers . . .

5. I envy . . .

6. I get hurt when . . .

7. I daydream about . . .

8. Few people know that I . . .

9. One thing I really dislike about myself is . . .

10. When I share my values with someone . . .

Source: Adapted from Egan, 1977

Based on your responses to the incomplete sentences, do you feel you engage in the right amount of self-disclosure? Too little? Too much?

In general, what prevents you from engaging in self-disclosure?

Are there particular topics on which you find it difficult to be self-disclosing?

Are you the recipient of much self-disclosure from others, or do people have difficulty opening up to you?

Social Avoidance and Distress Scale

INSTRUCTIONS

The statements below inquire about your personal reactions to a variety of situations. Consider each statement carefully. Then indicate whether the statement is true or false in regard to your typical behavior. Record your responses (true or false) in the space provided on the left.

THE SCALE

_____1. I feel relaxed even in unfamiliar social situations.

_____2. I try to avoid situations which force me to be very sociable.

_____ 3. It is easy for me to relax when I am with strangers.

_____ 4. I have no particular desire to avoid people.

_____ 5. I often find social occasions upsetting.

_____ 6. I usually feel calm and comfortable at social occasions.

_____ 7. I am usually at ease when talking to someone of the opposite sex.

_____ 8. I try to avoid talking to people unless I know them well.

_____ 9. If the chance comes to meet new people, I often take it.

_____10. I often feel nervous or tense in casual get-togethers in which both sexes are present.

_____11. I am usually nervous with people unless I know them well.

_____12. I usually feel relaxed when I am with a group of people.

_____13. I often want to get away from people.

_____14. I usually feel uncomfortable when I am in a group of people I don't know.

_____15. I usually feel relaxed when I meet someone for the first time.

_____16. Being introduced to people makes me tense and nervous.

_____17. Even though a room is full of strangers, I may enter it anyway.

_____18. I would avoid walking up and joining a large group of people.

_____19. When my superiors want to talk with me, I talk willingly.

_____20. I often feel on edge when I am with a group of people.

_____21. I tend to withdraw from people.

_____22. I don't mind talking to people at parties or social gatherings.

_____23. I am seldom at ease in a large group of people.

_____24. I often think up excuses in order to avoid social engagements.

_____25. I sometimes take the responsibility for introducing people to each other.

_____26. I try to avoid formal social occasions.

_____27. I usually go to whatever social engagements I have.

_____28. I find it easy to relax with other people.

SCORING THE SCALE

The scoring key is reproduced below. You should circle your true or false response each time it corresponds to the keyed response below. Add up the number of responses you circle, and this total is your score on the Social Avoidance and Distress (SAD) Scale. Record your score below.

1. False	8. True	15. False	22. False
2. True	9. False	16. True	23. True
3. False	10. True	17. False	24. True
4. False	11. True	18. True	25. False
5. True	12. False	19. False	26. True
6. False	13. True	20. True	27. False
7. False	14. True	21. True	28. False

MY SCORE_____

Source: Watson & Friend, 1969

WHAT THE SCALE MEASURES

As its name implies, this scale measures avoidance and distress in social interactions. David Watson and Ronald Friend (1969) developed the scale to assess the extent to which individuals experience discomfort, fear, and anxiety in social situations and the extent to which they therefore try to evade many kinds of social encounters. To check the validity of the scale, they used it to predict subjects' social behavior in experimentally contrived situations. As projected, they found that people who scored high on the SAD Scale were less willing than low scorers to participate in a group discussion. The high scorers also reported anticipating more anxiety about their participation in the discussion than the low scorers. Additionally, Watson and Friend found a strong negative correlation (–.76) between the SAD and a measure of affiliation drive (the need to seek the company of others).

INTERPRETING YOUR SCORE

Our norms are based on data collected by Watson and Friend (1969) on over 200 university students.

NORMS

High score:	16–28
Intermediate score:	6–15
Low score:	0–5

How Do You Relate to Friends?

The following questions (adapted from Egan, 1977) are designed to help you think about how you deal with friendships.

1. Do you have many friends or very few?

2. Whether many or few, do you usually spend a lot of time with your friends?

3. What do you like in other people—that is, what makes you choose them as friends?

4. Are the people you go around with like you or different from you? Or are they in some ways like you and in other ways different? How?

5. Do you like to control others, to get them to do things your way? Do you let others control you? Do you give in to others much of the time?

6. Are there ways in which your friendships are one-sided?

Source: Adapted from Egan, 1977

Self-Report Jealousy Scale

INSTRUCTIONS

The following scale lists some situations in which you may have been involved, or in which you could be involved. Rate them with regard to how you would feel if you were confronted with the situation by circling a number that corresponds to one of the reactions shown on the right. Do not omit any items.

0	1	2	3	4
Pleased	Mildly upset	Upset	Very upset	Extremely upset

THE SCALE

_____1. Your partner expresses the desire that you both develop other romantic relationships.

_____2. Your partner spends increasingly more time at work with a co-employee you feel could be sexually attractive to your partner.

_____3. Your partner suddenly shows an interest in going to a party when he or she finds out that someone will be there with whom he or she has been romantically involved with previously.

_____4. At a party, your partner hugs someone other than you.

_____5. You notice your partner repeatedly looking at another.

_____6. Your partner spends increasingly more time in outside activities and hobbies in which you are not included.

_____7. At a party, your partner kisses someone you do not know.

_____8. Your boss, with whom you have had a good working relationship in the past, now seems to be more interested in the work of a co-worker.

_____9. Your partner goes to a bar several evenings without you.

_____10. Your partner recently received a promotion, and the new position requires a great deal of travel, business dinners, and parties, most of which you are not invited to attend.

_____11. At a party, your partner dances with someone you do not know.

_____12. You and a co-worker worked very hard on an extremely important project. However, your boss gave your co-worker full credit for it.

_____13. Someone flirts with your partner.

_____14. At a party, your partner repeatedly kisses someone you do not know.

_____15. Your partner has sexual relations with someone else.

_____16. Your brother or sister is given more freedom, such as staying up later, or driving the car.

_____17. Your partner comments to you on how attractive another person is.

_____18. While at a social gathering of a group of friends, your partner spends little time talking to you, but engages the others in animated conversation.

_____19. Grandparents visit your family, and they seem to devote most of their attention to a brother or sister instead of you.

_____20. Your partner flirts with someone else.

_____21. Your brother or sister seems to be receiving more affection and/or attention from your parents.

_____22. You have just discovered your partner is having an affair with someone at work.

_____23. The person who has been your assistant for a number of years at work decides to take a similar position with someone else.

_____24. The group to which you belong appears to be leaving you out of plans, activities, etc.

_____25. Your best friend suddenly shows interest in doing things with someone else.

Source: Bringle et al., 1979

SCORING THE SCALE

Give yourself 4 points for every item where your response was "extremely upset," 3 points for every item where your response was "very upset," 2 points for every item where your reponse was "upset," 1 point for every item where your response was "mildly upset," and 0 for every item where your response was "pleased." In other words, add up the numbers you circled. The total is your score on the Self-Report Jealousy Scale.

MY SCORE_____

WHAT THE SCALE MEASURES

As its name indicates, this scale measures your tendency to get jealous in a variety of situations. It does not measure romantic jealousy exclusively, as ten of the items relate to nonromantic jealousy. Hence, it assesses jealousy in a general way, with a heavy emphasis on romantic relationships.

This scale, which was developed by Bringle, Roach, Andle, and Evenbeck (1979), has adequate test-retest reliability. Correlations with other personality traits have been examined in efforts to demonstrate its validity. People who score high on the scale tend to have low self-esteem, to be anxious, to see the world in negative terms, and to feel they have little control over their lives. These are interesting preliminary findings, although more research is needed to better validate this instrument.

INTERPRETING YOUR SCORE

Our norms are based on the sample of 162 college students studied by Bringle et al. (1979). They may be inappropriate for older, nontraditional college students.

NORMS

High score:	83–100
Intermediate score:	59–82
Low score:	0–58

How Do You Behave in Intimate Relationships?

The following questions (adapted from Corey & Corey, 1986, 1997) are intended to make you think about how you act in intimate relationships. They are designed for people in "couple-type" relationships, but if you are not currently involved in one, you can apply them to whatever relationship is most significant in your life (for instance, with your parents, children, or best friend).

1. What are some sources of conflict in your relationship? Check any of the following items that apply to you, and list any other areas of conflict in the space provided.

_____Spending money

_____Use of free time

_____What to do about boredom

_____Investment of energy in work

_____Interest in others of the opposite sex

_____Outside friendships

_____Wanting children

_____How to deal with children

_____Differences in basic values

_____In-laws

_____Sexual needs and satisfaction

_____Expression of caring and loving

_____Power struggles

_____Role conflicts

_____Others (list below)

2. How do you generally cope with these conflicts in your relationship? Check the items that most apply to you.

_____By open dialogue

_____By avoidance

_____By fighting and arguing

_____By compromising

_____By getting involved with other people or in projects

List other ways in which you deal with conflicts in your relationships.

Source: Adapted from Corey & Corey, 1986, 1997

3. List some ways in which you've changed during the period of your relationship. How have your changes affected the relationship?

4. How much do you need (and depend upon) the other person? Imagine that he or she is no longer in your life, and write down how your life might be different.

Personal Attributes Questionnaire

INSTRUCTIONS

The items below inquire about what kind of a person you think you are. Each item consists of a pair of characteristics, with the letters A–E in between. For example:

Not At All Artistic A   B   C   D   E   Very Artistic

Each pair describes contradictory characteristics—that is, you cannot be both at the same time, such as very artistic and not at all artistic.

The letters form a scale between the two extremes. You are to enter a letter that describes where you fall on the scale. For example, if you think you have no artistic ability, you would enter A. If you think you are pretty good, you might enter D. If you are only medium, you might enter C, and so forth.

THE SCALE

____1. Not at all aggressive   A   B   C   D   E   Very aggressive

____2. Not at all independent   A   B   C   D   E   Very independent

____3. Not at all emotional   A   B   C   D   E   Very emotional

____4. Very submissive   A   B   C   D   E   Very dominant

____5. Not at all excitable in a major crisis   A   B   C   D   E   Very excitable in a major crisis

____6. Very passive   A   B   C   D   E   Very active

____7. Not at all able to devote self completely to others   A   B   C   D   E   Able to devote self completely to others

____8. Very rough   A   B   C   D   E   Very gentle

____9. Not at all helpful to others   A   B   C   D   E   Very helpful to others

___10. Not at all competitive   A   B   C   D   E   Very competitive

___11. Very home oriented   A   B   C   D   E   Very worldly

___12. Not at all kind   A   B   C   D   E   Very kind

___13. Indifferent to others' approval   A   B   C   D   E   Highly needful of others' approval

___14. Feelings not easily hurt   A   B   C   D   E   Feelings easily hurt

___15. Not at all aware of feelings of others   A   B   C   D   E   Very aware of feelings of others

___16. Can make decisions easily   A   B   C   D   E   Has difficulty making decisions

___17. Gives up very easily   A   B   C   D   E   Never gives up easily

___18. Never cries   A   B   C   D   E   Cries very easily

___19. Not at all self-confident   A   B   C   D   E   Very self-confident

___20. Feels very inferior   A   B   C   D   E   Feels very superior

___21. Not at all understanding of others   A   B   C   D   E   Very understanding of others

___22. Very cold in relations with others   A   B   C   D   E   Very warm in relations with others

___23. Very little need for security   A   B   C   D   E   Very strong need for security

___24. Goes to pieces under pressure   A   B   C   D   E   Stands up well under pressure

Source: Spence & Helmreich, 1978

SCORING THE SCALE

The Personal Attributes Questionnaire (PAQ) is made up of three 8-item subscales, but we are only going to compute scores for two of these subscales, so the first step is to eliminate the 8 items from the unused subscale. Put an X in the spaces to the left of the items for the following items: 1, 4, 5, 11, 13, 14, 18, and 23. These items belong to the subscale that we won't be using, and they can be ignored. Of the remaining items, one (item 16) is reverse-scored as follows. If you circled A, enter 4 in the space to the left of item 5; if you circled B, enter 3; if you circled C, enter 2; if you circled D, enter 1; and if you circled E, enter 0. All the rest of the items are scored in the following manner: A = 0, B = 1, C = 2, D = 3, and E = 4. Based on the responses you circled, enter the appropriate numbers for the remaining items in the spaces to the left of the items.

The next step is to compute your scores on the femininity and masculinity subscales of the PAQ. To compute your score on the *femininity* subscale, add up the numbers next to items 3, 7, 8, 9, 12, 15, 21, and 22, and enter your score in the space below. To compute your score on the *masculinity* subscale, add up the numbers next to items 2, 6, 10, 16, 17, 19, 20, and 24, and enter your score in the space below.

MY SCORE ON THE FEMININITY SUBSCALE _____

MY SCORE ON THE MASCULINITY SUBSCALE _____

WHAT THE SCALE MEASURES

Devised by Janet Spence and Robert Helmreich (1978), the PAQ assesses masculinity and femininity in terms of respondents' self-perceived possession of various personality traits that are stereotypically believed to differentiate the sexes. The authors emphasize that the PAQ taps only limited aspects of sex roles: certain self-assertive/instrumental traits traditionally associated with masculinity and certain interpersonal/expressive traits traditionally associated with femininity. Although the PAQ should not be viewed as a global measure of masculinity and femininity, it has been widely used in research to provide a rough classification of subjects in terms of their gender-role identity. As explained in your text, people who score high in both masculinity and femininity are said to be androgynous. People who score high in femininity and low in masculinity are said to be feminine sex-typed. Those who score high in masculinity and low in femininity are characterized as masculine sex-typed, and those who score low on both dimensions are said to be sex-role undifferentiated.

INTERPRETING YOUR SCORE

You can use the chart shown below to classify yourself in terms of gender-role identity. Our norms are based on a sample of 715 college students studied by Spence and Helmreich (1978). The cutoffs for "high" scores on the masculinity and femininity subscales are the medians for each scale. Obviously, these are very arbitrary cutoffs, and results may be misleading for people who score very close to the median on either scale, as a difference of a point or two could change their classification. Hence, if either of your scores is within a couple of points of the median, you should view your gender-role classification as very tentative.

	My Femininity Score	
	High (above median) 22-32	Low (at or below median) 0-21
My Masculinity Score High (above median) 24-32	Androgynous	Masculine sex-typed (if male) or cross-sex-typed (if female)
Low (at or below median) 0-23	Feminine sex-typed (if female) or cross-sex-typed (if male)	Undifferentiated

MY CLASSIFICATION _____

What percentage of subjects falls into each of the four gender-role categories? The exact breakdown will vary depending on the nature of the sample, but Spence and Helmreich (1978) reported the following distribution for their sample of 715 college students.

CATEGORY	Males	Females
Androgynous	25%	35%
Feminine	8%	32%
Masculine	44%	14%
Undifferentiated	23%	18%

How Do You Feel About Gender Roles?

1. Can you recall any experiences that were particularly influential in shaping your attitudes about gender roles? If yes, give a couple of examples.

2. Have you ever engaged in cross-sex-typed behavior? Can you think of a couple of examples? How did people react?

3. Do you ever feel restricted by gender roles? If so, in what ways?

4. Have you ever been a victim of sex discrimination (sexism)? If so, describe the circumstances.

5. How do you think the transition in gender roles has affected you personally?

Death Anxiety Scale

INSTRUCTIONS

If a statement is true or mostly true as applied to you, circle T. If a statement is false or mostly false as applied to you, circle F.

THE SCALE

T F 1. I am very much afraid to die.

T F 2. The thought of death seldom enters my mind.

T F 3. It doesn't make me nervous when people talk about death.

T F 4. I dread to think about having to have an operation.

T F 5. I am not at all afraid to die.

T F 6. I am not particularly afraid of getting cancer.

T F 7. The thought of death never bothers me.

T F 8. I am often distressed by the way time flies so very rapidly.

T F 9. I fear dying a painful death.

T F 10. The subject of life after death troubles me greatly.

T F 11. I am really scared of having a heart attack.

T F 12. I often think about how short life really is.

T F 13. I shudder when I hear people talking about a World War III.

T F 14. The sight of a dead body is horrifying to me.

T F 15. I feel that the future holds nothing for me to fear.

SCORING THE SCALE

The scoring key is reproduced below. You should circle your response each time it corresponds to the keyed response below. Add up the number of responses that you circle. This total is your score on the Death Anxiety Scale.

1. True	6. False	11. True
2. False	7. False	12. True
3. False	8. True	13. True
4. True	9. True	14. True
5. False	10. True	15. False

WHAT THE SCALE MEASURES

Virtually no one looks forward to death, but some of us fear death more than others. Some people are reasonably comfortable with their mortality, and others have difficulty confronting the idea that someday they will die. This scale measures the strength of your anxiety about death. When investigators do research on how age, sex, religion, health, and other variables are related to death anxiety, they use scales such as this one.

Developed by Lonetto and Templer (1983), the Death Anxiety Scale has excellent reliability. Demonstrating the validity of a scale that measures death anxiety is complex, but the scale does correlate with other measures of death anxiety. Scores also correlate positively with clinical judgments of subjects' death anxiety.

INTERPRETING YOUR SCORE

Our norms are based on a sample of 1271 adults (parents of adolescents) cited by Lonetto and Templer (1983). Although females tend to score a little higher than males on this scale, we have reported combined norms.

Norms

High score:	9–15
Intermediate score:	4–8
Low score:	0–3

MY SCORE_____

Source: Lonetto & Templer, 1983

How Do You Feel About Age Roles?

1. Discuss how your behavior has been restricted by age roles. (For example, has anyone ever told you to "act your age"?)

2. Have you ever been a victim of ageism? If so, describe.

3. Give an example of how a social clock has influenced your behavior.

4. List seven adjectives that you associate with being elderly.

5. Given the information reviewed in the chapter, do you feel that the adjectives you chose are accurate descriptions of the elderly? To what degree do they reflect stereotypes of the elderly?

Assertive Job-Hunting Survey

INSTRUCTIONS

This inventory is designed to provide information about the way in which you look for a job. Picture yourself in each of these job-hunting situations and indicate how likely it is that you would respond in the described manner. If you have never job-hunted before, answer according to how you would try to find a job. Please record your responses in the spaces to the left of the items. Use the following key for your responses:

1	2	3	4	5	6
Very unlikely	Somewhat unlikely	Slightly unlikely	Slightly likely	Somewhat likely	Very likely

THE SCALE

_____1. When asked to indicate my experiences for a position, I would mention only my paid work experience.

_____2. If I heard someone talking about an interesting job opening, I'd be reluctant to ask for more information unless I knew the person.

_____3. I would ask an employer who did not have an opening if he knew of other employers who might have job openings.

_____4. I downplay my qualifications so that an employer won't think I'm more qualified than I really am.

_____5. I would rather use an employment agency to find a job than apply to employers directly.

_____6. Before an interview, I would contact an employee of the organization to learn more about that organization.

_____7. I hesitate to ask questions when I'm being interviewed for a job.

_____8. I avoid contacting potential employers by phone or in person because I feel they are too busy to talk with me.

_____9. If an interviewer were very late for my interview, I would leave or arrange for another appointment.

_____10. I believe an experienced employment counselor would have a better idea of what jobs I should apply for than I would have.

_____11. If a secretary told me that a potential employer was too busy to see me, I would stop trying to contact that employer.

_____12. Getting the job I want is largely a matter of luck.

_____13. I'd directly contact the person for whom I would be working, rather than the personnel department of an organization.

_____14. I am reluctant to ask professors or supervisors to write letters of recommendation for me.

_____15. I would not apply for a job unless I had all the qualifications listed on the published job description.

_____16. I would ask an employer for a second interview if I felt the first one went poorly.

_____17. I am reluctant to contact an organization about employment unless I know there is a job opening.

_____18. If I didn't get a job, I would call the employer and ask how I could improve my chances for a similar position.

_____19. I feel uncomfortable asking friends for job leads.

_____20. With the job market as tight as it is, I had better take whatever job I can get.

_____21. If the personnel office refused to refer me for an interview, I would directly contact the person I wanted to work for, if I felt qualified for the position.

_____22. I would rather interview with recruiters who come to the college campus than contact employers directly.

_____23. If an interviewer says "I'll contact you if there are any openings," I figure there's nothing else I can do.

_____24. I'd check out available job openings before deciding what kind of job I'd like to have.

_____25. I am reluctant to contact someone I don't know for information about career fields in which I am interested.

SCORING THE SCALE

To score this scale, you have to begin by reversing your responses on 18 of the items. On these items, convert the response you entered as follows: 1 = 6, 2 = 5, 3 = 4, 4 = 3, 5 = 2, and 6 = 1. The items to be reversed are 1, 2, 4, 5, 7, 8, 10, 11, 12, 14, 15, 17, 19, 20, 22, 23, 24, and 25. After making your reversals, add up the numbers that you have recorded for the 25 items on the scale. This total is your score on the Assertive Job-Hunting Survey.

MY SCORE _____

Source: Becker et al., 1980

WHAT THE SCALE MEASURES

Developed by Heather Becker, Susan Brown, Pat LaFitte, Mary Jo Magruder, Bob Murff, and Bill Phillips, this scale measures your job-seeking style (Becker, 1980). Some people conduct a job search in a relatively passive way—waiting for jobs to come to them. Others tend to seek jobs in a more vigorous, assertive manner. They act on their environment to procure needed information, obtain helpful contacts, and get their foot in the door at attractive companies. This scale measures your tendency to pursue jobs assertively.

Test-retest reliability for this scale is reasonable (.77 for an interval of two weeks). The scale's validity has been supported by demonstrations that subjects' scores increase as a result of training programs designed to enhance their job-hunting assertiveness. Also, those who have job-hunted before tend to score higher than those who have never job-hunted.

INTERPRETING YOUR SCORE

Our norms are based on a sample of college students who had applied to a university counseling center for career-planning assistance.

NORMS

High score:	117–150
Intermediate score:	95–116
Low score:	0–94

What Do You Know About the Career That Interests You?

Important vocational decisions require information. Your assignment in this exercise is to pick a vocation and research it. You should begin by reading some occupational literature. Then you should interview someone in the field. Use the outline below to summarize your findings.

1. *The nature of the work.* What are the duties and responsibilities on a day-to-day basis?

2. *Working conditions.* Is the working environment pleasant or unpleasant, low-key or high-pressure?

3. *Job entry requirements.* What kind of education and training are required to break into this occupational area?

4. *Potential earnings.* What are entry-level salaries, and how much can you hope to earn if you're exceptionally successful?

5. *Opportunities for advancement.* How do you "move up" in this field? Are there adequate opportunities for promotion and advancement?

6. *Intrinsic job satisfactions.* What can you derive in the way of personal satisfaction from this job?

7. *Future outlook.* How is supply and demand projected to shape up in the future for this occupational area?

Sexuality Scale

INSTRUCTIONS

For the 30 items that follow, indicate the extent of your agreement or disagreement with each statement, using the key shown below. Record your responses in the spaces to the left of the items.

+2	+1	0	−1	−2
Agree	Slightly agree	Neither agree nor disagree	Slightly agree	Disagree

THE SCALE

_____1. I am a good sexual partner.

_____2. I am depressed about the sexual aspects of my life.

_____3. I think about sex all the time.

_____4. I would rate my sexual skill quite highly.

_____5. I feel good about my sexuality.

_____6. I think about sex more than anything else.

_____7. I am better at sex than most other people.

_____8. I am disappointed about the quality of my sex life.

_____9. I don't daydream about sexual situations.

_____10. I sometimes have doubts about my sexual competence.

_____11. Thinking about sex makes me happy.

_____12. I tend to be preoccupied with sex.

_____13. I am not very confident in sexual encounters.

_____14. I derive pleasure and enjoyment from sex.

_____15. I'm constantly thinking about having sex.

_____16. I think of myself as a very good sexual partner.

_____17. I feel down about my sex life.

_____18. I think about sex a great deal of the time.

_____19. I would rate myself low as a sexual partner.

_____20. I feel unhappy about my sexual relationships.

_____21. I seldom think about sex.

_____22. I am confident about myself as a sexual partner.

_____23. I feel pleased with my sex life.

_____24. I hardly ever fantasize about having sex.

_____25. I am not very confident about myself as a sexual partner.

_____26. I feel sad when I think about my sexual experiences.

_____27. I probably think about sex less often than most people.

_____28. I sometimes doubt my sexual competence.

_____29. I am not discouraged about sex.

_____30. I don't think about sex very often.

SCORING THE SCALE

To arrive at your scores on the three subscales of this questionnaire, transfer your responses into the spaces provided below. If an item number has an R next to it, this item is reverse-scored, so you should change the + or − sign in front of the number you recorded. After recording your responses, add up the numbers in each column, taking into account the algebraic sign in front of each number. The totals for each column are your scores on the three subscales of the Sexuality Scale. Record your scores at the bottom of each column.

Sexual Esteem	Sexual Depression	Sexual Preoccupation
1. _____	2. _____	3. _____
4. _____	5.R _____	6. _____
7. _____	8. _____	9.R _____
10.R _____	11.R _____	12. _____
13.R _____	14.R _____	15. _____
16. _____	17. _____	18. _____
19.R _____	20. _____	21.R _____
22. _____	23.R _____	24. _____
25.R _____	26. _____	27.R _____
28.R _____	29.R _____	30.R _____
_____	_____	_____

Source: Snell & Papini, 1989

WHAT THE SCALE MEASURES

Developed by William Snell and Dennis Papini (1989), the Sexuality Scale measures three aspects of your sexual identity. The Sexual Esteem subscale measures your tendency to evaluate yourself in a positive way in terms of your capacity to relate sexually to others. The Sexual Depression subscale measures your tendency to feel saddened and discouraged by your ability to relate sexually to others. The Sexual Preoccupation subscale measures your tendency to become absorbed in thoughts about sex on a persistent basis.

This is a relatively new scale that has not yet been the subject of extensive research. Internal reliability is excellent. Thus far, the scale's validity has been examined through factor analysis, which can be used to evaluate the extent of overlap among the subscales. The factor analysis showed that the three subscales do measure independent aspects of one's sexuality.

INTERPRETING YOUR SCORES

Our norms are based on Snell and Papini's (1989) sample of 296 college students drawn from a small university in the Midwest. Significant gender differences were found only on the Sexual Preoccupation subscale, so we report separate norms for males and females only for this subscale.

NORMS

Sexual Esteem Both Sexes	Sexual Depression Both Sexes	Sexual Preoccupation	
		Males	Females
High Score			
+14 to +20	+1 to +20	+8 to +20	−1 to +20
Intermediate Score			
0 to +13	−12 to 0	−2 to +7	−10 to −2
Low Score			
−20 to −1	−20 to −13	−20 to −3	−20 to −11

How Did You Acquire Your Attitudes About Sex?

1. Whom do you feel was most important in shaping your attitudes regarding sexual behavior (parents, teachers, peers, early girlfriend or boyfriend, and so forth)?

2. What was the nature of their influence?

3. If the answer to the first question was *not* your parents, what kind of information did you get at home? Were your parents comfortable talking about sex?

4. In childhood, were you ever made to feel shameful, guilty, or fearful about sex? How?

5. Were your parents open or secretive about their own sex lives?

6. Do you feel comfortable with your sexuality today?

Chronic Self-Destructiveness Scale

INSTRUCTIONS

For each of the following statements, indicate the degree to which the statement describes you. Record your responses in the spaces provided by writing in a letter from A to E, using the following scale: **A** expresses *strongest agreement*; **B** expresses *moderate agreement*; **C** indicates that you're *unsure or undecided*, or that it's a toss-up; **D** expresses *moderate disagreement*; **E** expresses *strongest disagreement*.

_____1. I like to listen to music with the volume turned up as loud as possible.

_____2. Life can be pretty boring.

_____3. When I was a kid, I was suspended from school.

_____4. I usually eat breakfast.

_____5. I do not stay late at school functions when I must get up early.

_____6. I use or have used street drugs.

_____7. I like to spend my free time "messing around."

_____8. As a rule, I do not put off doing chores.

_____9. Riding fast in a car is thrilling.

_____10. I tend to defy people in authority.

_____11. I have a complete physical examination once a year.

_____12. I have done dangerous things just for the thrill of it.

_____13. I am the kind of person who would stand up on a roller coaster.

_____14. I do not believe in gambling.

_____15. I find it necessary to plan my finances and keep a budget.

_____16. I let people take advantage of me.

_____17. I hate any kind of schedule or routine.

_____18. I usually meet deadlines with no trouble.

_____19. I am familiar with basic first-aid practices.

_____20. Even when I have to get up early, I like to stay up late.

_____21. I insist on traveling safely rather than quickly.

_____22. I have my car serviced regularly.

_____23. People tell me I am disorganized.

_____24. It is important to get revenge when someone does you wrong.

_____25. Sometimes I don't seem to care what happens to me.

_____26. I like to play poker for high stakes.

_____27. I smoke over a pack of cigarettes a day.

_____28. I have frequently fallen in love with the wrong person.

_____29. I just don't know where my money goes.

_____30. Wearing a helmet ruins the fun of a motorcycle ride.

_____31. I take care to eat a balanced diet.

_____32. Lots of laws seem made to be broken.

_____33. I am almost always on time.

_____34. I like jobs with an element of danger.

_____35. I often walk out in the middle of an argument.

_____36. Often I don't take very good care of myself.

_____37. I rarely put things off.

_____38. I speak my mind even when it's not in my best interest.

_____39. I usually follow through on projects.

_____40. I've made positive contributions to my community.

_____41. I make promises that I don't keep.

_____42. An occasional fight makes a guy more of a man.

_____43. I always do what my doctor or dentist recommends.

_____44. I know the various warning signs of cancer.

_____45. I usually call a doctor when I'm sure I'm becoming ill.

_____46. I maintain an up-to-date address/phone book.

_____47. I sometimes forget important appointments I wanted to keep.

_____48. I drink two or fewer cups of coffee a day.

_____49. It's easy to get a raw deal from life.

_____50. I eat too much.

_____51. I often skip meals.

_____52. I don't usually lock my house or apartment door.

_____53. I know who to call in an emergency.

_____54. I can drink more alcohol than most of my friends.

_____55. The dangers from using contraceptives are greater than the dangers from not using them.

_____56. I seem to keep making the same mistakes.

_____57. I have my eyes examined at least once a year.

_____58. I lose often when I gamble for money.

_____59. I leave on an outdoor light when I know I'll be coming home late.

_____60. Using contraceptives is too much trouble.

_____61. I often use nonprescription medicines (aspirin, laxatives, etc.).

_____62. I do things I know will turn out badly.

_____63. When I was in high school, I was considered a good student.

_____64. I have trouble keeping up with bills and paperwork.

_____65. I rarely misplace even small sums of money.

_____66. I am frequently late for important things.

_____67. I frequently don't do boring things I'm supposed to do.

Source: Kelley et al., 1985

_____68. I feel really good when I'm drinking alcohol.

_____69. Sometimes when I don't have anything to drink, I think about how good some booze would taste.

_____70. It's really satisfying to inhale a cigarette.

_____71. I like to smoke.

_____72. I believe that saving money gives a person a real sense of accomplishment.

_____73. I like to exercise.

SCORING THE SCALE

The scoring instructions are different for males and females. The 73 items you just responded to actually represent two overlapping 52-item scales for each sex.

Females: Convert your letter responses to numbers from 1 to 5 (A = 1, B = 2, C = 3, D = 4, E = 5) for items 5, 8, 11, 15, 18, 19, 21, 22, 31, 33, 37, 39, 40, 43, 44, 45, 46, 53, and 63. Convert your responses in the opposite way (A = 5, B = 4, C = 3, D = 2, E = l) for items 1, 2, 6, 7, 9, 10, 12, 16, 17, 20, 23, 24, 25, 26, 28, 29, 30, 32, 36, 38, 41, 47, 49, 54, 56, 58, 60, 61, 62, 64, 66, 67, and 69. You should now have 52 items for which you have a number recorded instead of a letter. Add up these numbers, and the total is your score on the Chronic Self-Destructiveness Scale (CSDS) .

Males: Convert your letter responses to numbers from 1 to 5 (A = 1, B = 2, C = 3, D = 4, E = 5) for items 4, 14, 18, 21, 22, 39, 40, 45, 48, 53, 57, 59, 63, 65, 72, and 73. Convert your responses in the opposite way (A = 5, B = 4, C = 3, D = 2, E = l) for items 2, 3, 10, 12, 13, 17, 25, 26, 27, 28, 29, 30, 32, 34, 35, 36, 41, 42, 47, 49, 50, 51, 52, 54, 55, 56, 58, 60, 62, 64, 66, 67, 68, 69, 70, and 71. You should now have 52 items for which you have a number recorded instead of a letter. Add up these numbers, and the total is your score on the Chronic Self-Destructiveness Scale (CSDS).

MY SCORE_____

WHAT THE SCALE MEASURES

Developed by Kathryn Kelley and associates (Kelley et al., 1985), this scale measures your tendency to behave in a self-destructive manner. Kelley et al. (1985) define chronic self-destructiveness as a generalized tendency to engage in acts that increase the likelihood of future negative consequences and/or decrease the likelihood of future positive consequences. In other words, chronic self-destructiveness involves behavior that probably will be detrimental to one's well-being in the long run. This self-destructive quality is viewed as an aspect of personality that may underlie a diverse array of counterproductive, often health-impairing habits.

In their initial series of studies, Kelley et al. (1985) administered their scale to 12 groups of undergraduates, a group of businesswomen, and a group of hospital patients. In comparison to people with low scores, high scorers on the CSDS were more likely to (a) report having cheated in classes, (b) have violated traffic laws, (c) indulge in drug or alcohol abuse meriting treatment, (d) recall a rebellious stage in adolescence, and (e) postpone important medical tests.

INTERPRETING YOUR SCORE

Our norms are based on 234 female and 168 male undergraduates studied by Kelley et al. (1985). In light of the age trends mentioned above, these norms may not be appropriate for older students.

NORMS

	Females	Males
High score	157–260	158–260
Intermediate score	105–156	97–157
Low score	52–104	52–96

How Do Your Health Habits Rate?

	Almost Always	Sometimes	Almost Never
EATING HABITS			
1. I eat a variety of foods each day, such as fruits and vegetables, whole-grain breads and cereals, lean meats, dairy products, dry peas and beans, and nuts and seeds.	4	1	0
2. I limit the amount of fat, saturated fat, and cholesterol I eat (including fat on meats, eggs, butter, cream, shortenings, and organ meats such as liver).	2	1	0
3. I limit the amount of salt I eat by cooking with only small amounts, not adding salt at the table, and avoiding salty snacks.	2	1	0
4. I avoid eating too much sugar (especially frequent snacks of sticky candy or soft drinks).	2	1	0

EATING HABITS SCORE:_____

	Almost Always	Sometimes	Almost Never
EXERCISE/FITNESS			
1. I maintain a desired weight, avoiding overweight and underweight.	3	1	0
2. I do vigorous exercises for 15 to 30 minutes at least three times a week (examples include running, swimming, and brisk walking).	3	1	0
3. I do exercises that enhance my muscle tone for 15 to 30 minutes at least three times a week (examples include yoga and calisthenics).	2	1	0
4. I use part of my leisure time participating in individual, family, or team activities that increase my level of fitness (such as gardening, bowling, golf, and baseball).	2	1	0

EXERCISE/FITNESS SCORE:_____

	Almost Always	Sometimes	Almost Never
ALCOHOL AND DRUGS			
1. I avoid drinking alcoholic beverages or I drink no more than one or two drinks a day.	4	1	0
2. I avoid using alcohol or other drugs (especially illegal drugs) as a way of handling stressful situations or the problems in my life.	2	1	0
3. I am careful not to drink alcohol when taking certain medicines (for example, medicine for sleeping, pain, colds, and allergies).	2	1	0
4. I read and follow the label directions when using prescribed and over-the-counter drugs.	2	1	0

ALCOHOL AND DRUGS SCORE:_____

WHAT YOUR SCORES MEAN:

9–10	Excellent
6–8	Good
3–5	Mediocre
0–2	Poor

Do any of your scores surprise you? Why?

Source: Adapted from the Department of Health and Human Services, 1981

Manifest Anxiety Scale

INSTRUCTIONS

The statements below inquire about your behavior and emotions. Consider each statement carefully. Then indicate whether the statement is generally true or false for you. Record your responses (true or false) in the spaces provided.

THE SCALE

_____ 1. I do not tire quickly.

_____ 2. I believe I am no more nervous than most others.

_____ 3. I have very few headaches.

_____ 4. I work under a great deal of tension.

_____ 5. I frequently notice my hand shakes when I try to do something.

_____ 6. I blush no more often than others.

_____ 7. I have diarrhea once a month or more.

_____ 8. I worry quite a bit over possible misfortunes.

_____ 9. I practically never blush.

_____ 10. I am often afraid that I am going to blush.

_____ 11. My hands and feet are usually warm enough.

_____ 12. I sweat very easily even on cool days.

_____ 13. Sometimes when embarrassed, I break out in a sweat that annoys me greatly.

_____ 14. I hardly ever notice my heart pounding, and I am seldom short of breath.

_____ 15. I feel hungry almost all the time.

_____ 16. I am very seldom troubled by constipation.

_____ 17. I have a great deal of stomach trouble.

_____ 18. I have had periods in which I lost sleep over worry.

_____ 19. I am easily embarrassed.

_____ 20. I am more sensitive than most other people.

_____ 21. I frequently find myself worrying about something.

_____ 22. I wish I could be as happy as others seem to be.

_____ 23. I am usually calm and not easily upset.

_____ 24. I feel anxiety about something or someone almost all the time.

_____ 25. I am happy most of the time.

_____ 26. It makes me nervous to have to wait.

_____ 27. Sometimes I become so excited that I find it hard to get to sleep.

_____ 28. I have sometimes felt that difficulties were piling up so high that I could not overcome them.

_____ 29. I must admit that I have at times been worried beyond reason over something that really did not matter.

_____ 30. I have very few fears compared to my friends.

_____ 31. I certainly feel useless at times.

_____ 32. I find it hard to keep my mind on a task or job.

_____ 33. I am unusually self-conscious.

_____ 34. I am inclined to take things hard.

_____ 35. At times I think I am no good at all.

_____ 36. I am certainly lacking in self-confidence.

_____ 37. I sometimes feel that I am about to go to pieces.

_____ 38. I am entirely self-confident.

SCORING THE SCALE

The scoring key is reproduced below. You should circle each of your true or false responses that correspond to the keyed responses. Add up the number of responses you circle, and this total is your score on the Manifest Anxiety Scale.

1. False	2. False	3. False	4. True	5. True
6. False	7. True	8. True	9. False	10. True
11. False	12. True	13. True	14. False	15. True
16. False	17. True	18. True	19. True	20. True
21. True	22. True	23. False	24. True	25. False
26. True	27. True	28. True	29. True	30. False
31. True	32. True	33. True	34. True	35. True
36. True	37. True	38. False		

MY SCORE_____

Source: Taylor, 1953

WHAT THE SCALE MEASURES

You just took a form of the Taylor Manifest Anxiety Scale (1953), as revised by Richard Suinn (1968). Suinn took the original 50-item scale and identified all items for which there was a social desirability bias (11) or a response set (1). He eliminated these 12 items and found that the scale's reliability and validity were not appreciably decreased. Essentially, the scale measures trait anxiety—that is, the tendency to experience anxiety in a wide variety of situations.

RESEARCH ON THE SCALE

Hundreds of studies have been done on the various versions of the Taylor Manifest Anxiety Scale. The validity of the scale has been supported by demonstrations that various groups of psychiatric patients score higher than unselected groups of "normals" and by demonstrations that the scale correlates well with other measures of anxiety. Although the Manifest Anxiety Scale is no longer a "state of the art" measure of anxiety, it is an old classic that is relatively easy to score.

INTERPRETING YOUR SCORE

Our norms are based on data collected by Suinn (1968) on 89 undergraduates who responded to the scale anonymously.

NORMS

High score:	16–38
Intermediate score:	6–15
Low score:	0–5

What Are Your Attitudes on Mental Illness?

1. List seven adjectives that you associate with people who are diagnosed as mentally ill.

2. If you meet someone who was once diagnosed as mentally ill, what are your immediate reactions?

3. List some comments about people with psychological disorders that you heard when you were a child.

4. Have you had any actual interactions with "mentally ill" people that have supported or contradicted your expectations?

5. Do you agree with the idea that psychological disorders should be viewed as an illness or disease? Defend your position.

Attitudes Toward Seeking Professional Psychological Help

INSTRUCTIONS

Read each statement carefully and indicate your agreement or disagreement, using the scale below. Please express your frank opinion in responding to each statement, answering as you honestly feel or believe.

0 = Disagreement
1 = Probable disagreement
2 = Probable agreement
3 = Agreement

THE SCALE

_____ 1. Although there are clinics for people with mental troubles, I would not have much faith in them.

_____ 2. If a good friend asked my advice about a mental health problem, I might recommend that he see a psychiatrist.

_____ 3. I would feel uneasy going to a psychiatrist because of what some people would think.

_____ 4. A person with a strong character can get over mental conflicts by himself, and would have little need of a psychiatrist.

_____ 5. There are times when I have felt completely lost and would have welcomed professional advice for a personal or emotional problem.

_____ 6. Considering the time and expense involved in psychotherapy, it would have doubtful value for a person like me.

_____ 7. I would willingly confide intimate matters to an appropriate person if I thought it might help me or a member of my family.

_____ 8. I would rather live with certain mental conflicts than go through the ordeal of getting psychiatric treatment.

_____ 9. Emotional difficulties, like many things, tend to work out by themselves.

_____ 10. There are certain problems that should not be discussed outside of one's immediate family.

_____ 11. A person with a serious emotional disturbance would probably feel most secure in a good mental hospital.

_____ 12. If I believed I was having a mental breakdown, my first inclination would be to get professional attention.

_____ 13. Keeping one's mind on a job is a good solution for avoiding personal worries and concerns.

_____ 14. Having been a psychiatric patient is a blot on a person's life.

_____ 15. I would rather be advised by a close friend than by a psychologist, even for an emotional problem.

_____ 16. A person with an emotional problem is not likely to solve it alone; he or she is likely to solve it with professional help.

_____ 17. I resent a person—professionally trained or not—who wants to know about my personal difficulties.

_____ 18. I would want to get psychiatric attention if I was worried or upset for a long period of time.

_____ 19. The idea of talking about problems with a psychologist strikes me as a poor way to get rid of emotional conflicts.

_____ 20. Having been mentally ill carries with it a burden of shame.

_____ 21. There are experiences in my life I would not discuss with anyone.

_____ 22. It is probably best not to know everything about oneself.

_____ 23. If I were experiencing a serious emotional crisis at this point in my life, I would be confident that I could find relief in psychotherapy.

_____ 24. There is something admirable in the attitude of a person who is willing to cope with his conflicts and fears without resorting to professional help.

_____ 25. At some future time I might want to have psychological counseling.

_____ 26. A person should work out his own problems; getting psychological counseling would be a last resort.

_____ 27. Had I received treatment in a mental hospital, I would not feel that it had to be "covered up."

_____ 28. If I thought I needed psychiatric help, I would get it no matter who knew about it.

_____ 29. It is difficult to talk about personal affairs with highly educated people such as doctors, teachers, and clergymen.

SCORING THE SCALE

Begin by reversing your response (0 = 3, 1 = 2, 2 = 1, 3 = 0) for items 1, 3, 4, 6, 8, 9, 10, 13, 14, 15, 17, 19, 20, 21, 22, 24, 26, and 29. Then add up the numbers for all 29 items on the scale. This total is your score. Record your score below.

MY SCORE_____

WHAT THE SCALE MEASURES

The scale assesses the degree to which you have favorable attitudes toward professional psychotherapy (Fischer & Turner, 1970). The higher your score, the more positive your attitudes about therapy. As we have discussed, there are many negative stereotypes about therapy, and many people are very reluctant to pursue therapy. This is unfortunate, because negative attitudes often prevent people from seeking therapy that could be beneficial to them.

NORMS

High score:	64–87
Medium score:	50–63
Low score:	0–49

Source: Fisher & Turner, 1970

What Are Your Feelings About Therapy?

The following questions are intended to help you examine your attitudes regarding professional psychotherapy.

1. If you have had any experience with mental health professionals, describe what it was like.

2. Based on your experience, would you recommend professional counseling to a friend?

3. List any considerations that might prevent you from seeking some form of therapy even if you felt a need or desire to do so.

4. If you were looking for a therapist, what criteria would you employ in making your choice?

5. Briefly describe what you would expect to get out of professional therapy or counseling.

REFERENCES

Anderson, N. H. (1968). Likableness ratings of 555 personality trait words. *Journal of Personality and Social Psychology, 9,* 272–279.

Barnes, G. E., & Vulcano, B. A. (1982). Measuring rationality independent of social desirability. *Personality and Individual Differences, 3,* 303–309.

Becker, H. A. (1980). The Assertive Job-Hunting Survey. *Measurement and Evaluation in Guidance, 13,* 43–48.

Bringle, R., Roach, S., Andler, C., & Evenbeck, S. (1979). Measuring the intensity of jealous reactions. *Catalogue of Selected Documents in Psychology, 9,* 23–24.

Burger, J. M. (1992). *Desire for control: Personality, social, and clinical perspectives.* New York: Plenum.

Burger, J. M., & Cooper, H. M. (1979). The desirability of control. *Motivation and Emotion, 3,* 381–393.

Corey, G., & Corey, M. S. (1986, 1997). *I never knew I had a choice* (3rd & 6th eds.). Pacific Grove, CA: Brooks/Cole.

Egan, G. (1977). *You and me: The skills of communicating and relating to others.* Pacific Grove, CA: Brooks/Cole.

Ellis, A. (1962). *Reason and emotion in psychotherapy.* Seacaucus, NJ: Lyle Stuart.

Ellis, A. (1973). *Humanistic psychotherapy: The rational-emotive approach.* New York: Julian Press.

Fischer, E. H., & Turner, J. L. (1970). Orientations to seeking professional help: Development and research utility of an attitude scale. *Journal of Consulting and Clinical Psychology, 35,* 82–83.

Gibb, B. (1964). *Test-wiseness as secondary cue response.* Unpublished doctoral dissertation, Stanford University, California.

Ickes, W., &. Barnes, R. D. (1977). The role of sex and self-monitoring in unstructured dyadic interactions. *Journal of Personality and Social Psychology, 35,* 315–330.

Infante, D. A., & Rancer, A. S. (1982). A conceptualization and measure of argumentativeness. *Journal of Personality Assessment, 46,* 72–80.

Kelley, K., Byrne, D., Przybyla, D. P. J., Eberly, C., Eberly, B., Greendlinger, V., Wan, C. K., & Gorsky, J. (1985). Chronic self-destructiveness: Conceptualization, measurement and initial validation of the construct. *Motivation and Emotion, 9,* 135–151.

Lonetto, R., &. Templer, D. I. (1983). The nature of death anxiety. In C. D. Spielberger & J. N. Butcher (Eds.), *Advances in personality assessment* (Vol. 3). Hillsdale, NJ: Erlbaum.

Miller, L. C., Berg, J. H., & Archer, R. L. (1983). Openers: Individuals who elicit intimate self-disclosure. *Journal of Personality and Social Psychology, 44,* 1234–1244.

Snell, W. E., Jr., & Papini, D. R. (1989). The sexuality scale: An instrument to measure sexual-esteem, sexual-depression, and sexual-preoccupation. *Journal of Sex Research, 26,* 256–263.

Snyder, M. (1974). Self-monitoring of expressive behavior. *Journal of Personality and Social Psychology, 30,* 526–537.

Spence, J. T., & Helmreich, R. L. (1978). *Masculinity and femininity: Their psychological dimensions, correlates, and antecedents.* Austin, TX: University of Texas Press.

Suinn, R. M. (1968). Removal of social desirability and response set items from the Manifest Anxiety Scale. *Educational and Psychological Measurement, 28,* 1189–1192.

Taylor, J. A. (1953). A personality scale of manifest anxiety. *Journal of Abnormal and Social Psychology, 48,* 285–290.

Watson, D. L., & Friend, R. (1969). Measurement of social-evaluative anxiety. *Journal of Consulting and Clinical Psychology, 33,* 448–57.

Weiten, W., Clery, J., & Bowbin, G. (1980, September). *Test-wiseness: Its composition and significance in educational measurement.* Paper presented at the meeting of the American Psychological Association, Montreal, Quebec.

Zuckerman, M. (1979). *Sensation seeking: Beyond the optimal level of arousal.* Hillsdale, NJ: Erlbaum.

CREDITS

This page constitutes an extension of the copyright page. We have made every effort to trace the ownership of all copyrighted material and to secure permission from copyright holders. In the event of any question arising as to the use of any material, we will be pleased to make the necessary corrections in future printings. Thanks are due to the following authors, publishers, and agents for permission to use the material indicated.

Page 9: From "The Desirability of Control," by J. M. Burger and H. M. Cooper, 1979, *Motivation and Emotion, 3*, 381–393. Copyright © 1979 Plenum Publishing. Reprinted by permission.

Page 13: From *Sensation Seeking: Beyond the Optimal Level of Arousal*, pp. 45–47, by M. Zuckerman (512–6). Copyright © 1979 by Lawrence Erlbaum Associates, Inc. Reprinted by permission.

Page 17: Reprinted from "Measuring Rationality Independent of Social Desirability," by G. E. Barnes and B. A. Vulcano, 1982, *Personality and Individual Differences, 3*, 303–309, with kind permission from Elsevier Science Ltd, The Boulevard, Langford Lane, Kidlington OX5 1GB, UK.

Page 21: From "Self-Monitoring of Excessive Behavior," by M. Snyder, 1974, *Journal of Personality and Social Psychology, 330*, 526–537. Copyright © 1974 by the American Psychological Association. Reprinted by permission.

Page 25: From "A Conceptualization and Measure of Argumentativeness," by D. A. Infante & A. S. Rancer, 1982, *Journal of Personality Assessment, 46*, 72–80. Copyright © Lawrence Erlbaum Associates, Inc. Reprinted by permission.

Page 29: From "Opener: Individuals Who Elicit Intimate Self-Disclosure," by L. C. Miller, J. H. Berg, & R. L. Archer, 1983, *Journal of Personality and Social Psychology, 6*, 123–124. Copyright © 1983 by the American Psychological Association. Reprinted by permission.

Page 31: Adapted from *You and Me: The Skills of Communicating and Relating to Others*, by G. Egan. Copyright © 1977 Brooks/Cole Publishing Co.

Page 33: From "Measurement of Social-Evaluative Anxiety," by D. L. Watson & R. Friend, 1969, *Journal of Consulting and Clinical Psychology, 33*, 448–457. Copyright © 1969 American Psychological Association. Reprinted by permission.

Page 35: Adapted from *You and Me: The Skills of Communicating and Relating to Others*, by G. Egan. Copyright © 1977 Brooks/Cole Publishing Co.

Page 37: From "Measuring the Intensity of Jealous Relationships," by R. Bringle, S. Roach, C. Andler, & S. Evenbeck, 1979, *Catalogue of Selected Documents in Psychology, 9*, 23–24. Copyright © 1979 by Select Press, San Rafael, CA. Reprinted by permission.

Page 39: Adapted from *I Never Knew I Had A Choice*, 3rd & 6th eds., by G. Corey and M. S. Corey. Copyright © 1986 & 1997 Brooks/Cole Publishing Co.

Page 41: From *Masculinity and Femininity: Their Psychological Dimensions, Correlates, and Antecedents*, by J. T. Spence and R. L. Helmreich. Copyright © 1978 University of Texas Press. Reprinted by permission.

Page 45: From "The Nature of Death Anxiety," by R. Lonetto and D. I. Templer. In C. D. Spielberger and J. N. Butcher (Eds.), *Advances in Personality Assessment* (Vol. 3), pp. 14–174. Copyright © 1983 Lawrence Erlbaum. Reprinted by permission of Donald I. Templer, California School of Professional Psychology.

Page 49: From *Assertive Job-Hunting Survey* (1980) by Heather Becker, Susan Brown, Pat Lafitte, Mary Jo Magruder, Bob Murff, & Bill Phillips. Instrument reproduced with permission of Heather Becker.

Page 53: From "The Sexuality Scale: An Instrument to Measure Sexual-Esteem, Sexual-Depression, and Sexual-Preoccupation," by W. E. Snell & D. R. Papini, 1989, *Journal of Sex Research, 26*(2), 256–263. Copyright © 1989 Society for Scientific Study of Sex. Reprinted by permission of the author.

Page 57: From "Chronic Self-Destructiveness: Conceptualization, Measurement, and Initial Validation of the Construct," by K. Kelley, D. Bryne, D. P. J. Przbyla, C. Eberly, B. Eberly, V. Greendinger, C. K. Wan, & J. Gorsky, 1985, *Motivation and Emotion, 9*(2). Copyright © 1985 by Plenum Publishing Company. Reprinted by permission.

Page 59: Adapted from "Health Style: A Self-Test," Washington, D.C.: U.S. Department of Health and Human Services, Public Health Service, PHS 81-50155, 1981.

Page 61: From "A Personality Scale of Manifest Anxiety," by J. A. Taylor, 1953, *Journal of Abnormal and Social Psychology, 48*, 285–290. Copyright © 1953 American Psychological Association.

Page 65: From "Orientations to Seeking Professional Help: Development and Research Utility of an Attitude Scale," by E. H. Fisher & J. L. Turner, 1970, *Journal of Consulting and Clinical Psychology, 35*, 82–83. Copyright © 1970 by the American Psychological Association. Reprinted by permission.

TO THE OWNER OF THIS WORKBOOK

We hope that you have found *Personal Explorations Workbook* for *Psychology Applied to Modern Life: Adjustment in the 90s, Fifth Edition,* useful. So that this workbook can be improved in a future edition, would you take the time to complete this sheet and return it? Thank you.

School and address: _____

Department: _____

Instructor's name: _____

1. What I like most about this workbook is: _____
_____
_____

2. What I like least about this workbook is: _____
_____
_____

3. My general reaction to this workbook is: _____
_____
_____

4. The name of the course in which I used this workbook is: _____
_____
_____

5. Were all the exercises in the workbook assigned for you to do? _____

   If not, which ones weren't? _____

6. In the space below, or on a separate sheet of paper, please write specific suggestions for improving this book and anything else you'd care to share about your experience in using the book.

_____
_____
_____
_____
_____
_____
_____
_____
_____
_____
_____
_____

Optional:

Your name: _____ Date: _____

May Brooks/Cole quote you, either in promotion for *Psychology Applied to Modern Life: Adjustment in the 90s, Fifth Edition,* or in future publishing ventures?

Yes: _____   No: _____

Sincerely,

Wayne Weiten
Margaret A. Lloyd

CUT ALONG DOTTED LINE

FOLD HERE

NO POSTAGE
NECESSARY
IF MAILED
IN THE
UNITED STATES

BUSINESS REPLY MAIL
FIRST CLASS   PERMIT NO. 358   PACIFIC GROVE, CA

POSTAGE WILL BE PAID BY ADDRESSEE

ATTN: *Wayne Weiten & Margaret A. Lloyd*

Brooks/Cole Publishing Company
511 Forest Lodge Road
Pacific Grove, California 93950-9968

FOLD HERE